A-MUSE: Myself

By Annalisa Bartlow

Createspace.com

Printed in the Untied Stated of America

ISBN 0-615-68382-7

I would like to dedicate this book and make a

special thanks to family for all their support.

Acknowledgements:

Without writing, without God giving me my gift, I would

not be able to express myself.

Special thanks to Ryan Callaway for giving the direction,

and encouragement to publish my own works.

Thank you to my parents for sticking with me no matter

how I act; what I have done where I have been; or what I

have become. They have always loved me just the same.

Every mistake, I have learned from, but I have also become

much closer to my parents.

Poem Index:

"It is not all art...some of it is rubbish, but when you look at a creation, and it gives you feelings and a connection; it is then, you know a piece of the artist's heart...Art is everything, everywhere."

---Annalisa Bartlow

The Wanderer:

Lost in darkness;

Confused by feelings.

All I can see is that I am heartless.

Ugly, monstrous, and with no appeal.

No light to safety;

No beauty to see.

Wishing for anything lovely;

Not caring what it be.

There is always hope.

Beyond my fears;

Only my hearts glow

Can evaporate my tears.

Confidence kills the pain.

It washes away the agony,

Of the lessons I have had to gain.

I will be stopped by no one.

<u>What this poem meant to me:</u>

I have always felt like I am searching in life. I am very confident I will find what I am looking for, and God will help me, but I am going in no particular direction. I feel like I was driven by fate to places in my life to meet people, and learn lessons. It humbled me, and I learned where I want to be in life. Wandering is not bad, just a process. I felt like a ship passing over troubled waters wandering towards my harbor.

Music:

Music is another language;

It is spoken only by the heart.

It instills emotion.

It fulfills the soul.

Music is an art;

It moves nations.

Bodies, and hearts.

It is easily made,

But, is not an easy trade.

It cannot be collected, nor made,

It is articulated, and never fades.

Music is versatile.

It comes in many forms.

It travels and moves everywhere.

Music is magic,

Another world emerges.

It conveys the mind.

Sacred, harsh, peaceful, spiritual,

And full of life.

Music, you cannot escape.

It is a path.

It is anger, love, passion, hope.

Let it consume you.

What this poem meant to me:

Music is a part of my life. I dedicate this poem to my father. I cannot play an instrument, or sing. I am what I call a "Simon", or critic in my family. I was not given much talent in music, but I see so much in music. I am just as much moved by music as my father. I was raised by two musicians. My father who played the drums since age three, could also play guitar, piano, and flute just to name a few. He put himself through college on gigs at local restaurants, bars, and other local towns. He also worked at a local music shop for a few years. He has played the drums at our church for over twenty years. My mother plays the guitar, piano, and violin. My little brother could pick up any instrument, and play a tune he had heard or remembered. My brother played the saxophone electric guitar, and drums. Even all of my grandparents played instruments. Of my whole family, I could not explain why I could not play. One Christmas my father got me a guitar. He knows I cannot play. To this day, I believe it is God sick joke. I cannot play anything, but I can listen to anyone of them play and truly critic the beats, rhythm, and harmony. Music is indirectly part of my life. In my inability to play music I have aspired to other arts that I excel in.

Facing the World:

Once upon a time…

There was a girl,

Who lived in fear.

She had no will,

But one year.

She brought herself out into the world.

Explored she did.

Her life became flustered and furled.

She learned and she hid.

The world was a scary place,

But she adapted.

Things she did saved her face.

She was impacted.

Now she is happy

She knew herself.

No longer sappy.

Adventures and trials she had;

It made her what she was.

Courage and trust of her heart;

Shaped her character.

<u>What this poem meant to me:</u>

I was once asked to tell a story. I wanted to be creative. I started rhyming and realized it was about me.

Lost:

So sick,

I feel like I am in a tornado.

Where I am from,

No one here knows.

Through a porthole I have come.

None of the magic shows.

Wandering through a dry dusty desert.

I carried a turtle.

Only cactus grew in the dirt.

The journey made me infertile.

Parched of thirst…

Barely breathing;

Not thinking at first.

I was certainly dreaming.

All I know was to walk forward.

I considered turning east.

But west was more forward.

The lake would help at least.

I wandered towards the lake.

It was a mirage.

I was annoyed by my mistake.

For it was a collage.

<u>What this poem meant to me:</u>

I wrote this when I was in Florida. I was transformed there. I learned very much on that treacherous journey. I was learning as I went. I hated my mistakes. I was in a lot of pain, but I saw the beauty in the darkness. I was not scared of the risk. I am glad I was fearless because it made life more manageable.

The Escape:

Weak, winded, and thirsty.

Barely breathing.

Writing to relieve my stress.

Heart is pounding;

Sitting on my bed,

Reading to escape,

Bundled up because I am always cold.

Difficult breathing.

Daydreaming, thinking.

Plotting,

So alone, don't know where home is,

Nauseous,

LOST!

Cold, so cold,

Unwanted worthless dreamer,

Emotional klutz;

Thinking of the near future.

Moving, separation, despair, panic, angles, school,

preparation.

Waiting,

Nervous withered old soul,

Rushing through a storm

<u>What this poem meant to me:</u>

This is from a time when I was running from my mistakes.

In my mind I was trying to figure out a way to get away

from the horrible situation I was in. The situations I

endured in Florida led to some interesting feelings. I was

suffering from severe manic depression, and was trying not

to ask for help. I have always been independent and have a

big problem with asking for help. It took me hitting rock

bottom emotionally for me to go to my mother and father. I

was never close to them until I was betrayed by my ex-

husband.

Colors:

`   Bunnies aren't blue

So I went with what I had

      Is that a haiku?

What this poem meant to me:

This was from a girl's night out (staying in). Sadly I am not close friends with all the people I was around when I wrote this, but I will never forget that fun night. We ranted, we gossiped, and laughed.

That's Haiku to You:

Tonight is girl's night

I love to drink beer with girls

I am super punk

What this poem meant to me:

I wrote everything on a napkin. I was goofing around with

word play and metering.

Food in the Night:

Bright and scary

The black olives are good

With the black berries

It was a night in,

Not out

What this poem meant to me:

This is from the girl's night out. At this point they realized I was writing. They started rambling, and whenever it rhymed I would take it down. I think it might have meant something to us that night, yet it is gibberish. The next morning it looked so stupid, but we were laughing so hard. I had so much fun and I will never forget the good times.

The Curse of the Central Valley:

In 1492, Columbus sailed the ocean blue.

To find a land, natives already knew.

Across the continent, on the perfect pacific shore,

There is a place you may have heard of before.

Amongst the fertile mountains and valley's; hugged by the deserts,

Lay the inescapable valley of the central coast.

With weather temperate, soil fertile, and there is an evil,

There is no escaping the curse of the Central Valley.

What this poem meant to me:

I wrote this about my town. I wrote it for everyone who has experienced the curse. I have a theory that it is cursed. It is very beautiful and bountiful. It is almost too good to be true. Strangely it is so hard to leave.

Maps:

Where will I hide now?

Am I loved without vow?

What road shall I continue through?

Shall I try anything bleed new?

I want a guide for my life.

A path written for my strife,

I want the world and more.

I want desires so that are far.

Far from here.

Far from me.

I know the way,

And obtained the directions.

What this poem meant to me:

Life after school has no general direction for anyone, and I

like being in control. Life will be hard, I just want to know:

Where? There is no real roadmap for life, but dreaming there is can be pleasant.

Heartless:

I have fallen into the deepest, darkest hole.

All I see is darkness.

And I have begun to find beauty in the gloom.

There is a glamor in pain and irritation.

I understand hate and adrenaline.

Actions are slow, and acceptance is chosen,

But darkness recklessly consumes me.

Pain is age, rage, revulsion, distrust, and horror.

Power corrupts and leads to pain, drowning in darkness.

When Pain consumes, one can only dream....

Dream, of being comforted;

There is no belief that there will be relief or healing,

So we just dream.

So, suffer we do, and suffer we must....

We are nothing more of life than that of disgust.

We trip and fall, hitting our head....

We fall, fall, fall down a crevice, a hovel...

Forever we fall,

Cuts, Bruises, broken bones,

Till out hearts can no longer bear it...

Each bit of pain replaces the last and matches it tenfold....

There is a lack of health...and existence...

In the end there is no way to heal.

Recognition of this is our suicide.

The body wants to fix it;

It still knows nothing but darkness and agony.

There is no way out but killing what makes us feel,

The core...

The source of life that is killing...torturing...

It sends something bad to the brain, and BANG....

No more woe.

Life is no longer yours, but you watch your frame...

Collected, cleaned, examined, and dressed up....

They lay you nicely in a box and morn over your soul...

If only they knew, all the aching was gone,

There would be no tears…..in your tailspin,

You set people on fire, and give them your pain.

Up in flames, this pain grows,

Somehow, they all know….

Your pain would not leave,

Now they will forever grieve…

What this poem meant to me:

This is about my depression…pain, and anger towards those who have been reckless with my heart. Through my depression I had many thoughts of suicide. Later I came to the conclusion that suicide is the most selfish thing a human could do. I have learned to express my pain through words and writing. Only there, the mind seems logical.

Thoughts, and Self-revelation:

We dance;

A step to the side.

If there is no harmony, there is pain;

I know it be true.

Without love there is no life.

Love and desire are so altered.

Respectful of darkness, pain and anger.

Accepting how it is to feel pain, and want to die.

Sometimes I feel it often.

It is my destiny, and it is not feared.

Fearful to hold a child in my womb;

It is not fanciful to destroy my body.

For happiness I would kill, if it we guaranteed.

It would be taken.

I do not know where I am going.

Sensations that I am rotting.

Already my mind it ruined.

There was a man cloaked.

He was a demon.

His stories exposed him.

He would die and I would be cursed to roam the world alone.

Tricked, sad, and in agony for eternity;

Rootless, from cycle to cycle.

As my ancestors were, I am a nomad.

A drifter;

I do not believe in life after this,

No one will survive this.

Traveling, without direction.

Observing the fiends he told me about.

I saw him; I know he is haunting me.

Haunting my every move made.

What this poem meant to me:

There are so many deep meanings to this poetry. It's about a few people. It is a lot about how, I feel like I have been fighting life and everything.

Incomplete Voyage:

So many doors.

So many paths…

No destination.

So lonely, and scared.

Don't know where I am going,

But know where I have been.

The past frightens me.

My youth is being sucked out of me.

Years are constant phases.

Yet it gets worse every season.

Life is a cliché.

It is intensifying my mind to a boiling point.

The mind is a cyclone.

People panic!

When worthless, there is no point.

Are you captivated?

For why I know not;

Which is unconceivable?

Nothing to give.

Nothing to take.

Dancing through time.

Life shoves me.

Journeys in memory and out of consciousness.

Uncertain of anything.

Here I am.

Naught, but I dream.

Dream that the pain will wash away.

And life could not get worse.

Cut me up,

Bury me.

Plant a garden, and watch it flourish on my frame.

Stories are all we are in the end;

Sometimes we are less than a footnote.

<u>What this poem meant to me:</u>

Fighting life, and going on; It is little bits of feelings that I have had. Life is a journey, and it is the pain that helps us grow.

Spirit:

I feel entirety.

So live on I do,

Kill me you will.

I dance over pain,

Through fire and agony;

I can move, swift and nimble.

Enjoy life.

Life burns me.

I am here.

High on insignificants;

Consequently suffering,

My insanity grows with every breath.

<u>What this poem meant to me:</u>

One needs to be positive, and in the right spirits.

Dreamer:

Dreams are all I know

Each night I go away

My favorite story in a way,

Neverland.

Life is but a dream within a dream.

What this poem meant to me:

Dreams are very important to me. We sleep for a third of

our life. As long as I can remember I have died in almost

every single dream. I find a lot of meaning in dreams.

Mystic:

Lighting laces the sky.

The only other light being the moon.

Everyone wants me.

It is suicide.

It's beyond madness.

There is no explaining exotic nature.

There is no control.

Insanity is beauty.

Skelton's follow me.

Though time, believing they know me.

Fairies smell trouble;

They rescue me.

Hiding from terror of society.

Marriage has ruined me.

Dancing in my bosom;

Where fairies find me; no one else does.

Do you dream?

Dream of being simple,

No fear.

There is negativity.

This is not me.

This is only time.

<u>What this poem meant to me:</u>

Time is to some degree of what we cannot see, but we can

observe. The solitary way we can perceive it is in cycles,

and by events being past, present. Time seems enchanted,

and perhaps sometimes that it is meticulous.

Infernos:

Like a raging fire,

Consuming everything in its path,

Attracted to life,

Eating whatever it can.

Destruction is the only remains.

Darkness falls.

Silence shouts to the skies.

Death gives birth to anew.

What this poem meant to me:

I was thinking about the fires the sweep across California

every year. In the year 2011 we did not have a fire season,

and this was odd to me, and it made me remember what it

looked like. The visual created this poem.

Divorcing Daemon:

Frivolous matters at hand.

Cut up your life.

And chop off my hand.

They hand the held true in strife.

I trusted you,

A demon;

Your only goal,

To consume my soul.

I will survive.

You will suffer.

You will have nothing.

To take from another.

Lower than dirt.

More revolting than disease.

You were a plague.

That will cease.

My heart was abused.

My mind was confused.

Now I am free.

That is something you will never see.

You said, 'I would never make it on my own'.

And yet, look at me now.

Crawled out of your pit in hell.

No longer under your spell.

<u>What this poem meant to me:</u>

I thought divorce was going to be easy. The process

irritated me. This anger spilled into a piece of paper on my

break at work one day.

Looking Around:

On wings of demons,

They fly like angels.

Manipulating the mind,

In no way are they kind.

No god will claim them,

Only foes among men.

Greed consumes,

Evil presumes.

Love does not overpower.

Fire dies like a flower.

They feed on love.

Destroying with a glove;

Slow, painful, withering,

Without life source they are suffering.

They are those,

That mimics the pose.

Hope and faith carries us.

A fairies flight…

A ghost's delight…

Pixies dance…

While witches chant.

Fire licks the sky,

A comfort to the eye.

The past horrors haunt us.

Only future holds confidence.

<u>What this poem meant to me:</u>

There are people in our lives who are mean, evil, and try to get what they want. I watch them every day, and it's entertaining. Colors of light bewitch and provoke our wits.

So Spins the Wheels:

Suffer we do.

Suffer we will.

Much is needed,

And so are you.

Where will we go?

What will we do?

Doesn't matter for me.

Neither for you;

Take your money.

Drain your pride.

Isn't this silly?

No, this is how it is done.

Fatally sad.

Far from the city.

Away from the clan.

When are we coming?

You know I am dying.

A joke or a lie.

That I will find.

You don't need me!

Scepters bear.

Life is frivolous.

From the towers we sing.

Denounce the horrible king.

The scene is sad.

Life has understudies.

Such is being.

I am filled with despair.

A deep ache.

Where will we go?

Where is the pleasure?

She is never here.

Pleasure is a life.

The life is the reproductions of where we make the sad.

Fretting…

Ares calls me.

The sound of war.

Life becomes empty.

Is it possible to survive?

Impossible!

We all die.

It turns my life.

Upside down.

She has a spell.

Aphrodite.

She sent me to hell

A scroll should be sung,

Not told.

Gloom is the way of justice.

If I sing a song..

A mystic song,

It is no diamond.

Here I sit,

Alone in a fit.

What this poem meant to me:

Life has many different elements to it. There is always to question of religion and how it reflects on life. Do gods play with the fates? How do we as people respond to everything logical and not? Life seems to spin on wheels, like a cycle.

Together Apart:

Long wait, over time,

Helping the heart understand.

One feeling blind;

The other at loves command.

Time slips as water over a rock.

Slow, but certain to make it...

Patience tests our heart.

We fly to each other like a magnet.

The embrace always sweet and perfect...

Love is appreciated more together.

Our bodies entwined around, exact.

Soft passionate kisses and hugs upon each other.

Sync with feelings and movement.

Hearts throbbing in harmony.

Never wanting to part.

Cherishing each second and being happy.

Time brings peace and rest.

We force ourselves to sleep.

Not wanting to part.

For on, come dreams, and a day deep.

<u>What this poem meant to me:</u>

This is about people I have loved and lost. It was simple feelings that I had at the time. It makes my head spin to believe I felt that way.

Managing Your Provender:

I have observed you like a specimen in a glass jar.

You are not what strangers believe you are.

Obsessions you follow.

Strangers you barely know…

Behind every back gossip is told.

Each word painfully more bold.

No respects are churned,

As the backs are turned.

Conceit, self-worth, and control have become your job.

You have become no more than a beast from a bog.

Fear surrounds you.

Words made on cue.

Possibly you feed off of pain,

As much as you can obtain.

Some inhabitants are wise,

Going where there is no despise.

Anger, scorn and hate!

What is our fate?

Run from a serpent swift and spiteful.

Never been near anything as frightful.

Or shall we risk fighting this monster?

Something, that should not be fostered;

Soon either way, you will suffocate.

Feeding on us will no longer be fate.

Will you drain our blood now?

For we are not going to bow...

We are not here living for you.

Nor 'er were the flowers for the dew.

Some things better with time,

But for you I would not lift a dime.

Lies are not worth chasing.

Not important to be facing.

What this poem meant to me:

Over the years, I have obtained the talent of not being fazed by others emotions and problems. It has taken a while to learn this. I am good at, not absorbing in their negativity, and just letting them be themself. The people I had been around for two years had been experiencing the pain of one of the group for some time. I have been asked why it does not affect me or hurt me. I took it home one night, and spilled onto a page what I hear and see. Verse is a good outlet to reverse feeling. I find it is far more effective than taking it back around the subject, for that self-perpetuates pain.

Drinking Beer & Riding Horses:

This be, the backbone.

Life, to forces.

A source, of men's thrones.

Love intense wound around,

The world it flies.

Through space, and

Around the sun as it dies.

Flowers grow like our hearts.

Toting away the minds, on carts.

Roots not so deep…

Leaves not so green…

Stalk no steep.

All be withering.

Animals riding forward.

Men intoxicated, in a bar.

Hormones party hard.

Boys riding in cars.

Coffee sobers.

Walks bring intimacy.

Dances of fire.

Love is felt though.

Thoughts of desire.

Emotion is a brew…

A child cries to her future.

Stay together from now.

Until forever; if only the imminent.

Could tell the past, life is harder.

Crouching low, time lingers.

Ready to pounce;

Knocking life from our fingers…

Never caring an ounce.

Pressed from the source.

Drained of its being.

Life has very little force.

Yet it overflows with feeling.

Dragons fly through the night sky.

Demons creep over the playground.

Cartoons waltz over a lazy screen.

Showing us monsters that have never been…

Mermaids lure sailors with song.

Strippers dance to lose their thong.

Lights flash and flicker…

Life is full of bicker.

Cope, cry, and manipulate.

Apples to pie, and so relate.

Is life in the hands of fate?

Phantoms fizz out all joy.

Eclipsing our hearts.

Playing the minds, like a toy.

Cruel world, so very smart!

Wind rushes, like a crush on the mind.

Lighting smashes though understanding.

Rage consumes, racing as a tornado.

Only peace can flood the mind.

What this poem meant to me:

No matter what we do in life, facts sit true, and

unchangeable. The myths, may be true, but they still sit

honest in our lives. Breathing or not, everything is

common; just as normal as drinking a beer, or riding a

horse.

Adoration:

Joyful in your arms.

Eternally in love.

In our friendship we have imbued.

I do not impugn my love for you.

The love you share inspires me to live.

Two twines dance through time.

Destiny fusing, binding a line.

Together stronger, lending each other's strength.

Love invincible!

You are my one desire.

What this poem meant to me:

I somewhat think this poem speaks for itself. It speaks of my love.

Night:

When the sun goes down,

The worlds at peace.

And the moon lights the earth,

With stars so bright and dreams a flight.

The world sits in harmony.

With Fluffy clouds and a cool breeze,

The sun has the time to sleep.

To prepare for the beautiful day ahead,

The world's at agreement.

What this poem meant to me:

It is the feeling that I get at dusk; that relaxing calming

part of the day when the Santa Ana Winds have just blown.

Life is so beautiful at this moment.

Life:

Lots of questions!

None of them answered…

Life is the biggest question of all!

Full of sadness, tears and sorrow!

My life is not my own.

Do I deserve what has been given to me?

The good and the bad?

It is all a voyage to the next division.

<u>What this poem meant to me:</u>

Life is rough. There are moments were there is confusion.

There is so much freedom to be shared that sometimes, it

can be a little overwhelming.

A Journey:

Sitting upon earths bed,

From, Mother Nature, fed.

A child walking in love…

Descending through life like a dove.

Fair in mind…

Heart, so kind.

Through trials and tribulation…

Misery stripped her of purification.

Anger wrapped her soul.

Pain became the goal.

Suffering consumed the mind.

To goodness she was blind.

Hope wrought new light.

To help fight for the right.

Conquest wore hell down…

Finally love had the crown.

<u>What this poem meant to me:</u>

I have seen myself turn many pages in life. Only once did I fully lose hope. It was a very long period in my life, and I can see where I lost myself, and where I came full circle.

Death:

I sing the song of death.

Coveted by the suffering…

Feared by power!

Death shows no mercy.

It knows no age or order.

Death knows when the time is right.

When she comes, don't put up a fight.

Death is not known or understood.

It is neither evil nor good.

Death hath no name,

Only has fear for its fame.

Many theories surround its being,

Nowhere is there proof of its failing.

Death of death itself would bring

A halt to the universe.

Dancing through time we would…

Never know what is worse.

Death steals.

Death gives peace.

Death brings forth new life.

It is the end of strife.

What this poem meant to me:

Benjamin Franklin once said, "Nothing in life is certain, but death and taxes". Death is something that brings full cycle to everything. With every beginning there is an end. Death is a very real. We may not be able to prove what is behind deaths doors, but we know it will all come to us. Do not fear death. This poem was me dwelling on what I see.

Seasons of Emotions:

Fear.

It consumes!

It eats away the soul.

It imprisons us.

Pain.

It is everywhere.

It surrounds us.

It hides us from the world.

Anger.

It arises like a flame.

When not controlled,

It overpowers us all.

It makes way for suffering and pain.

Revenge.

It solves nothing.

It can never fully be achieved.

It smothers the heart.

It is never just.

Love.

Is indescribable.

It is boundless, and uncontainable.

It multiplies.

Peace.

Being impossible.

Yet it is a decadent dream.

A magical thought.

The only feeling we can have.

Only existing in one's soul,

But never between mankind.

Kindness.

A rarity.

Incredibly amazing.

Fills the heart with joy.

<u>What this poem meant to me:</u>

I sat one day and reflected on feelings that I was having

that day. I broke it down more so, and thought: they are

just feelings. Do we every just think about the essence of

the feelings themselves?

Creative Maker

Flung through liquid…

Spun, over the universe.

On my mother's wheel;

The clay spins.

Directing hands press,

Fingers fold the skin.

Bones push the mold,

Carefully she lets it set.

Time relaxes the being.

The frame fires into a fullness.

Through the flames, and frequencies.

It takes form.

The being is real and solid.

Mother loves it, and gives it life.

Shades licks the clay with each stoke.

Deposits of ink are thin.

Passion finishes the figure!

So is the master's work...

Never a coincidence, but art!

An effort of love, exhaled to life.

What this poem meant to me:

I feel that my mom is one of the most creative people I know. We took pottery, and while watching her, made me feel she could create anything. I can see the love she put into her work, just like she put into me.

Thank you for reading my book.

It is my reflection on the world, that I see.

www.ingramcontent.com/pod-product-compliance
Lightning Source LLC
Chambersburg PA
CBHW021208020426
42331CB00003B/255